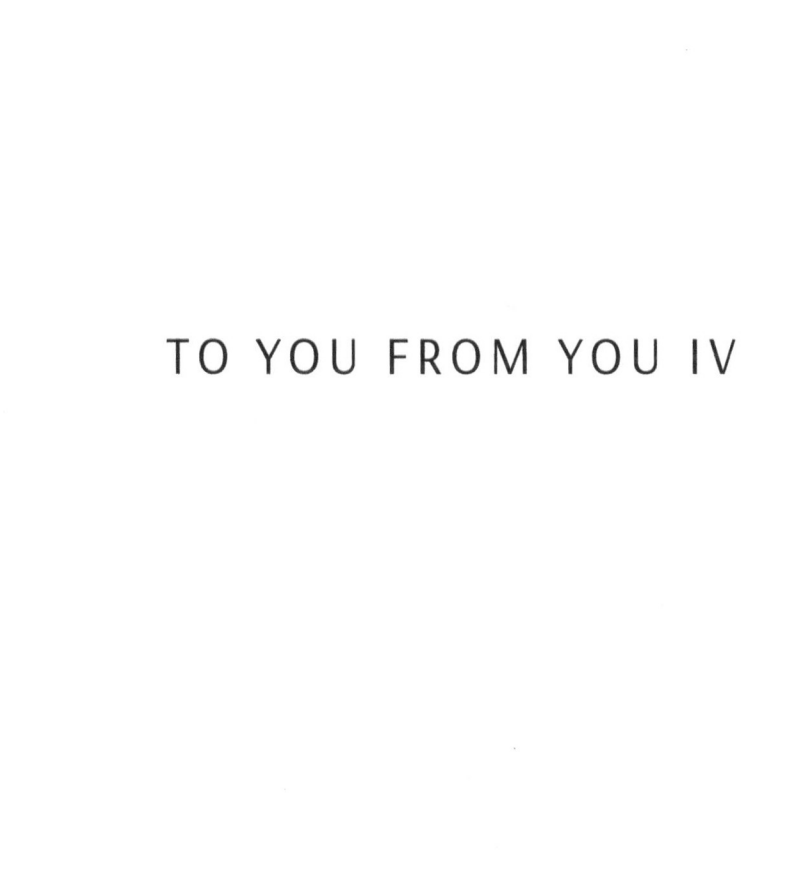

TO YOU FROM YOU IV

TABLE OF CONTENTS

Love Proven
Nuclear Shield
Structured Focus
Seasonal Story
Locus of Control
Stratospeed
Transient Soothing
Sturdy Grace
Vector Victory
Clipper Creature
Watchful Brink
Glean Fit
Emergent Convergence
Electric Wheel
Fear Not, Brave Heart
Serene Placement
Cumbia
Fractal Details
High Regards
Zipline Adventures
Faithful Hour
Second Sight
Probiotic Infusion
Gratitude of Expression
Better Than Fun, True Joy

Featured Faith
Peak Jubilee
Return of the Titans
Toll Taken
We can
Focused Fortune
Resonant Aura
Shimmer Glimmer
Joint Practice
Exceptional Fortress
High Caliber
Hard Love
Mysterious Enigma
Seventy Seven
Hmm...
Prudent Truce
Good Gracious
Stellation Constellation
Quantum Entanglement
Purple Lavender
Memory Recall
Forge Ahead
Honorable Gene
Grit Gears
Transcendent Affections
Faithful Endurance

Bout' Time
Synonym Characteristics
Drum Roll
Focal Point
Sophia
Strawberry Lemonade
Erg Origins
Chosen Determinism
Tranquility
Spring Sane
Joy Triumph
Mighty Will
Brotherhood
Lucky We
Yee Wee Knee
River Pebbles
Carried Field
Keen Force
Níκη

FARAH ALQATTAN

TO YOU FROM YOU IV

GRIT GEARS

DEDICATION

WORDS FROM THE AUTHOR

To the future,

There's a journey ahead. One that may demand of you and from you. There is no telling what will be around the corner. The strength of your faith amidst all you weather will bring tranquility and serenity to your experience. When you've come to face any fears, know, what's within your heart will shine brighter in the face of the dark. Plant kindness and peace wherever your steps lead you.

Remember, keep a grateful heart of appreciation, especially in the space of unknowingness.

This series is a sacred harvest to you and all you grow through. Never doubt how much you are loved and protected. Cheering you on!

With love,
Sourceful soul and family

p.s. It's possible to overcome and believe in goodness, for goodness sake!

Copyright© 2024 by Farah Alqattan

All rights reserved. No part of this book may be reproduced in any manner whatsoever without written permission except in the case of brief quotations embodied in critical articles and reviews.

Print Version: 2
Print ISBN: 979-8-9881785-3-8
Library of Congress Control Number: 2024918426
For permission and media, contact: farahalqattan.author@gmail.com
Author Instagram: farahalqattanofficial
Publisher Instagram: Rwhpublishing

Rwh Publishing LLC produces creative content by artists who aim to uplift humanity and change lives for the better.

Love Proven

*This bright sky
Even in dark times
There are others besides us who shine with insights*

*Don't doubt the story
Stemming from beginnings
Learned conditioning*

*It takes time to build
Not only the empire
But character within*

*Seeing higher above the world
Within, through spirit,
homes and temples*

*You've walked in a classroom and learned new subjects
Biology, chemistry, fitness
Teaching of the physical
But with time, the mind will crave the spiritual*

*May it be this or another message
Remember to be present*

Exercise patience
Give grace and compassion,
to see the signals today
Figuring this puzzle out, takes energy, focus, and courage

Be quick to forgive, so it doesn't sponge
Time and attention
Because of what was

Keep striving, steady pace
Harmony inner essence
Beauty

Planting more than flowers
Also within,
a special place,
a kingdom

Away from animalistic tendencies that seek attention
'More for me'

Instead of leaning into sincerity,
for life that's happening

Walk in joy, here it is
In your mind, you lead the way

Nuclear Shield

And after all days
Passing into years
The years into decades
The decades into lifetimes
Those lifetimes into ages
Generations
All turning into pages

How many are there?

Gracious soul
See you within your enemy, ill will be no more

That within the written text or genetics
Sequence of operation
Kindness, coded

A process
Within a system
A truthful foundation
Kingdom function

So what will this build for you?
Will it be on the outside or mental?
Beyond the virtual
Locked within the heart
Waiting to be discovered

So unlock the truth as this written
You've got permission

Let compassion undo the harm
Utter peace in infrastructure of design

Oh let it outpour
Even through the tears and wars

The love
The triumph
Overcomings

True victory beyond the horizons
Truth sending foundations

A happy home
Fortune of joy

Structured Focus

May we be honest
Giving due care
Caring
Not only of thyself but those beside us still here

The ones that made their way out to help
Early days, when we fought them
Just to feel egotistical

The ones trying even when they're hated
When falsehood is propagated
Either in private discussions
Or the virtual,
stemming from harmful stimulus and assumptions

The ones trying to help humanity
Without violence
Or words of weapons
Careful in choosing
Peaceful utterance

Oh be gentle, ways
Due care for the day
For peaceful becomings

Many will also choose
Regardless of the enticement
From other rationals
At times could be nationals
A mode of operation that refuses to see different
Perhaps set aside ego
To see and be with spirit

Without the constructs
What do they see?
What surfaces within their feels?
Is it love or kindness?
Or does it feel heat and fuel in hateness?
Does the hurt come about?
From the inside to the ones beside us

Distinguish the altitude
And the negative attitudes
Where are you headed?
Perhaps primary mathematics
Giving clues
Know the trajectory and be in your victory too

Positive or a negative force
See, fly like an eagle

Feel yourself coming home,
truth shelter,
better than before

Seasonal Story

Come up above
Into the potential
Progress between the occurrences
In an instance
Integrity
Doing the right thing
Between the stimulus
At times away from all you see

Take a pause
Think it through
Dichotomies of red or blue
Look here what a white canvas can bring
Third option, of the unseen

Often times, two options are presented
But hone down choice theory
Derive and think outside the box
Bring creative solutions and truthful understanding, to help

It can be a bake shop, sharing with your community
A little more healthy
Or a doctor that takes his time
Really inventories the symptoms of the frowns

In the pocket of interpretation
How well is our nation?
Look within
Making the difference

Locus of Control

Has experience tainted vision?
Because of upbringing
Or can a heart-beat with rhythm to help
Set aside those hurtful things

It's going to take every single one of us
To make this populus blossom
Not in fame or material luxury
But the heart, overflowing with laughter

Away from mental operations
Depression from senseless expressions
Away from complaints and false comparison
Just because of what is seen out in nature

Give and add
Even if you weren't given hope

Exponential development
Learning new perspectives
That of biology
Organics
And spirit
Soulful radiance

Stratospeed

Don't spend time in hate
Choices of yesterday
Focus attention on inner blossoming
Peacefulness

There's a mess
Sure
When the trash is not filtered

That of expression
Learned from propagated falsehoods

Where is all the attention spent?
What's the outlook?
Who's narrating?
Is it this love or hurt becomings?

Where will the energy be transferred?
Not created
Be humble with your propagation

Be honest
Not outside but within
Write thoughts
Write them out
Look
Intently
See what's in the heart

With time, we'll soon realize
It was the right moment,
to do different
Turning the dial, to peacefulness

Transient Soothing

*Subjectivity can cloud perception
In heat of moments, justifying*

*Don't fall for the illusions
Being, brought down
Aim for positive expression,
to get your crown*

*And soon, see for yourself
Abundance outflowing from within*

*Making a world of a difference
Through to the hearts of others near
Away from illness, hurt feelings, or greed*

*Casting out the hate and hurt hasting
Pretty soon all the pain extinguishing*

"What will remain, if we don't keep doing the same?"

*Armor of love
For family and friends*

*Generations
Outlasting*

Worthwhile joy filled existence

<u>Sturdy Grace</u>

*Oh sunshine
Here it is
Beyond the distance of doubts and embedded fears

All the worries that sept in at night
They be gone with each word written

Away from the mind and heart
No fear, soulfulness
Steadfast love
Significance

Don't let the thoughts drag you down
Here, take these scissors cut the crap out

Let this written, uplift you
Holding a handout for you
Come clear and be near
That which sees
Heartfelt
Sincere*

Breathe and let worries go
Never grow

Give water to your body to flourish
Growing confidence
Exercise
More than just tongues in misjudgments

You didn't come here on your own
Full of immunity
Don't weaken by abusing the senses
Thus, attract the harming

From risk behavior, orchestrated out in the open
Even when all you've wanted was a sense of belonging

Be cautious friend,
things are not what they seem
Prompt Engineering
Enticement
Negative energy at times bracelets

Vector Victory

Lean on this
Coming from wisdom

You've got gifts, yes you do
Believe
Believe
You will get through

You're a blessing here in this sphere
Work in the development created
Transfer away the heat
Never bury
Yourself under defeats
Or your neighbor for luxury, just to succeed
Give compassion and kindness
You're abundant

Give love and patience
Look how things will build you up
Not yet materialistically, but within your heart
So fortunate

Clipper Creatures

The past is history
Leave it where it needs to be

Why is the past occupying the present moment
Look now, what's surrounding you?
Why are you living back there?

The past won't propel
So look forward, don't walk backwards

Don't
Ruminate
Over those hurtful things
Captured thoughts
Open the door
Let them walkout

Clip it
Cast it
Bring it under your feet
Crush it
Never feel defeat

Do it physically
And observe
What will manifest within your spirit

You are wholesome
Feeling light
Even if you don't see your own might

Don't let the past dim your shine
Or the way you can help humanity rise

You are a winner
Better believe
In your given foundation
A beautiful design
Cells and mind
Victory, built
Each day, deciding "I won't give up. There is more to us"

So, clean yourself up
Not only physically but also inside
"How dirty are my thoughts?"

This won't mislead you
Building up
Higher inside
Climb the ladder

Marketing may tug at the senses
At times causing the loss of common sense
But this here, wisdom
Giving sacredness

In the sun
Or the mountains
Near the river
Or the Ocean
Energy shared
So decide, "How will I lead?"
Easily, up above
Not over someone else, but thyself

Watchful Brink

*You may find yourself almost down and out
Remember to keep a grateful heart
Give the unexpected
A smile
"We're full of heart with richness inside us"*

*Don't be taken or brought down,
when things are taken away from you
Sit here
Victory fulfilled
Power of attitude*

*So do different
Not yielding
Yelling at others just to make a point won't get even*

*Your attitude determines your altitude
Did they not clue you?
The physics and mathematics
Mixed with spirit
Optimal perspective, leading
Above all the hate into heaven*

*They may try to count you out
Count on this
Bet on spirit and angels
Leading the way*

*Beyond infrastructure or the planet
In the unseen
Winning*

*Pretty soon
You'll be making millions
Smile, don't frown
Even if the physical has shown no evidence*

*Smile dear friend,
smile
Joyus life is happening*

*And pretty soon it will change
Coming home
To a kingdom
That looks out for a friend
Not scoped to only value the materialistic*

*Valuing the truth,
intrinsic connection, for those beside you*

Glean Fit

Remember this
Character is important
So choose now, how will you show up?
Here, now, is the power
Lifeful gift
Hope sprinkled

Attributes of strength through tough times
A bit of intelligence reading non-fiction

A whole lot of patience
And forgiveness, through all the hate
Consciously choosing, even through the pain

Even with the wars on the news, enticing fears
It's so hard to grow
Beyond the shackles of the feels

Oh it takes so little
To be so special
-Observe-
Be yourself
Authentic
Not pressured to mimic what's presented

You are so loved
Never forgotten
You are more than a body made to consume
Bring here, faith and love
Making nations blossom
Not in the infrastructure but the heart
Hardened people will grow more soft

Remember, who you are
Love
Even when you had to face the shocks
You are not alone
Choose to be better into betterment
Full armor through conscious effort

Emergent Convergence

You're allowed to have reactions
Heated
Heightened temperaments
Heat of emotions
Fueling fire

But why burn out?
A family and tribe
Lookout
That's not a coolant

But this, here
brimming bringing healing

Take a moment
A time out,
before concluding or character attacking

There have been numerous instances
Even stimulus's
Triggering thoughts
But, where is the heart?
True love within
Residing, above all the hateness

The one facing you is not at fault
The senses are part of design
Domino effect
Mirror neurons
When we could be asking better questions

"What's the norm?"
"What are the subcultures breeding?"
"How are things operating or engineered?"
"Who's really at fault here?"

So don't blame anyone for how they're moving
Seek understanding

Move with compassion, love
Exercise grace
Give the unexpected
Silence is golden

It's okay to get it wrong
Dont argue because it will reaffirm
False narratives, within

Away from our heavenly foundation,
looking out for fellows near

Learn and transform the hurt
Shift perspective to help them see their own good

Beyond the easy way, to give up the false idols
A reminding of our modesty
Here in our kingdom
Life forms giving nourishment
Remembering the outlook, without any platforms
Raising up matter in front of you
Distracting eyes from seeing truth of silence

Electric Wheel

The best of us is in the rest of us
Within the heart
So is thy brother
Who may have been left out to die in the fire

Ways away
Beyond the atlantic
At least you've got shelter here
Where is the compassion?

Yes, how brave are they?
Facing storms without preparation
Experiencing it raw and bare
Through time and space

How great is it?
To be in the land of the Americas?
Military operation
Structure and order
Ensuring freedom

While people are enslaved to their senses
At times each person learning their nudges
Through inhibitions
It is important to know high distinctions and difference

If you see the patterns
Not only the data science
Intuitive
Explaining mysteries
The occurrence through situations
Propagated stimulus's
Valued math
But who here has taken time to understand the soulful essence?

You are being protected in ways unseen
Don't brush off the hunches just to feel good
Check-in with yourself
Ask questions
Elevate, here
Not only in the physical but suffering

"Why do I feel the way I do?"
"Where did it stem from?"
"Is it true rooted nature or learned conditioning?"

Fear Not, Brave Heart

You are loved beyond this page or any book
Things expressed by others can add to it
Or hinder perception
Even marketing can make you doubt design
Thinking of injecting to look more beautiful

But you've been glowing
It's the truth
We've all felt the love given
From source

That is the true beauty
Really it is
We don't see any blemishes
Loving your essence

All that really matters is the glimmer
How well you speak, of yourself and another near
Even in privacy

You've got armor of everlasting love
Beauty
Don't let others sink you
Come
Hear this truth

"You're safe"
There are so many with dark circles
At times having a pimple
Having sun spots and wrinkles too

Send gratitude to the cells
For having given beautiful skin
Olive oil, anti inflammatory

You will see,
love outshining from within you,
when you get smart and think through

All the blemishes gone
Exercising, full breathing
Giving healthy epidermis

Serene Placement

Become the truth
And see what will become of you
Calmness ways paving the path
Poised in unraveling times

Even when everyone around you is puzzled,
'How are they doing it?'
'Where do they get it from?'
And you will look not outside but only within your conscience

Reminding others, there's so much love and hope here
All we need to do is choose it

Even through the fears
Conditioning
The climates or the weather
The objects and projections reinforcing
You stand firm to not be swayed,
"Lets see if truth and love makes a worldwide difference"

We're in it together
Do the counts
Being fear-less
Embracing with a braveheart
True Courage

WOW-Zee

Sand storms
Spending more
Where is the investment?
Is it something that dries others out?
Or brings water feeling refreshed?
Not physically but within
How are people being nourished?

The easy road is fulfilling
The body
Materialistic
More for me

So lean on physics and take time
Learn so many topics
Putting the work becoming intelligent

Don't run away from responsibility
But to it
Honored
Respect and power

Put more tools under your belt
Invest in yourself
Prepare to help your nation
Through health and science
At least you won't be one of the problems

Yes, respectful and diligent
Floods of virtues into bloodstreams
Leading more than just your own life
Humanity, through the times

Cumbia

The day to day
Even the screams
More toys, for me

The children radical
Conditioned
7 or 11
Even at 50
Materialistically
Thinking objects will reflect spirit essence

The physical may eclipse
Trying to fit in
Know, true worth
Don't sink in the chase
Idolizing
Fiending just to feel
Walking the terrain
A sense of glory from the products to feel famous

So let all who need it, roam on through
Explorer adventures
Until they realize their spirit potential

Fractal Details

We will build it
Quality

Aiming to do the best
With all the tools and resources given
Excellence
Walking above the hardships

At times, tears may stream
If we're watching what's on TV
Triggering to think thoughts not circulated
From the inside of our spirit

So let's see what this here will surface
Triggering joy and peacefulness

A true friend sharing hope and upliftment
Without trying to pull and tug at your feet
To sink and bring you down under
Go on, feel bad
Trauma bonding
Insecurities, exploited
For a trophy or a dollar
This author here, refuses to let you fall or sink down under

So leave that space
Negativity,
is not where we're meant to be
Shame or hate
Putting anyone down
Step here, come up above into the haven

Nature is beaming with joy here today
Life given from source, shining
The only requirement, is to breathe
Eliminating disrespect, seeing others just as worthy

So cheer up
Buttercup
Don't give up
Not inside you
Not within the heart

Knock Knock
Are you still there?
Loving altitude
Victory
You are the true fortune

See us rising
So beautiful
Without greed
Fulfilling

They'll be wondering,
"How is it possible?"
"They didn't even use marketing or algorithms to reinforce clickbait behavior"

Little do they know the power endowed
In spirit and angels

See for yourself
How a true heart will always help
Through to generations, like never before

Not in consumption
Value of fame by those who deem this production is sweet to reel
Reinforcing harmful behavior

All the science has been there
Pointing the way away from the hurting

Healthy
Education
Giving foundations
Seems like they skipped the classrooms

<u>High Regards</u>

What was that?
Isn't it always something
or the other
This person
-rawr-
Fear
Look here
Give me your attention and focus
Captivating the audience

Something to talk about
Babyl for hours
Building more than just mindsets
Greed and hatefulness
Against nations and friends

Even the drama showcased on TV
Bad this or that
Fighting for attention
Not a modest operation

Learn the philosophy early on
Even John Locke expressed,
through the pages,
purpose of language
So it doesn't go about
Killing others in blood sports
Hurt and falsehood
We need to exercise purpose,
'Essay Concerning Human Understanding'

Oh how beautiful
Language
If used for the right purpose
Bringing forth healing
For peace and breathing
Giving true meaning

Zipline Adventures

Nectar of fresh fruit
Without the fried food
Moderation, a key

The body has been designed to withstand toxins
Without abuse
Sucrose, fructose, and glucose

Don't consume blindly
Just because it tastes good
It may help instantaneous
Stimulating the parasympathetic system
But pretty soon you'll notice the difference
Sluggish
Weak and tiredness
Not authentic fuelness
To keep holyship moving

Learn the endocrine
Jumping up in excitement
Compounded interest

Invest in yourself
Pouring fitness
Input and output
Pioneers

Better aim for longevity
Of who you'll children will become to be

Faithful Hour

Trust
Don't gloat in ego
Inflated
'Look at me'
Look at these objects making me feel worthy

Objectifying the experience
Can sink us down under
Falling for illusions
Calibrating comparisons

Envy too

So use each product and service
As a token of appreciation
Develop others up,
in kindness not comparison

Even within the mind,
thinking you're better than

Than those who came here naked,
having nothing but a sourceful gift

Currency call of 'The mighty will'
So look here, who's more fortunate?

Intrinsic faithful inspiration

Second Sight

Intention has impact
We will make a difference
So aim to leave and ripple
Something beautiful

Spoken words
Forgiveness and truce

Let toxic grudges and resentment leave
Evict them outside of the home in the mental

Let yourself reside with clarity
Clean home and space
Positive reinforcement
Letting go of frustrations

Be cautious,
what are words amplifying?
Every word carries a frequency
Practice more silence here

In a noisy world,
rise higher through the wavelength
Higher vibration
Let these planted words have you see

Even through the pressure
Royal
Living with pure intentions

Probiotic Infusion

Be patient
It's easy
Give space
Focus on chi

Oh the life force within you
The beautiful energy
Aura
Shining
Felt by those beside you

So don't let others project the hate onto you
What they sell
May sink you down under

Oh look now, beneath
All those empty canisters
That are sold on the shelf
Making others feel drowsy and inhibited
Leading neural pathways
To weakness

But this here, lifting higher
Better know, "Their souls will not be in the fire"

Gratitude of Expression

Thank you service workers
Not only in the food and beverage
But also the military
Mothers and fathers
In construction and plumbing
Keeping our streets clean

Thank you for spending days while others developed
In this generation or the others
Giving hope and second chances
While young grew in changes

You are a treasure
True gift
Don't feel ashamed for having less

You are held in high worth and regard
Even through eyes reading this, here and now

We give thanks
Believe
All across the worlds
Markets shared in diversity
Even driving uber or taxis

The beauty of the stylists
Engineers
Architects
Foreign service workers
Developing infrastructure

Thanks to those on the back-end
Administrative professionals
Servanthood
Grocery attendants

Thank you
This is has been overdue
Thank you
And all you do
We're truly grateful, for you

Better than Fun, True Joy

Regardless of things expressed
A true heart will never give up
Believe
Believe
We will make it better

-breathe-

We're climbing up higher
No fear
Truth spoken here
Hear

It's going to take faith
We've got plenty of it
Full heart and well of courage

Bold faith
Offering
Gliding
Upward

Above the world
Until all the hurt becomes sand castles

A different narrative
A new story
Change mode of operation
Through mindfulness
Planting love here

Willing it into existence
Blooming like the seasons
Beyond the oceans

In the mind, resides a key
Transient transfer
"It's possible, no fear"

Indeed it is
With a will from heaven building others temples

Don't shy away from the opportunity
Take up the sword
Love sharpened

Inside of harmony
Breaking the chains
That kept darkness within the mind,
through the spirits who may be struggling

Breakaway
Here comes the light
Full of insight, no fright

You are born free with love
So act like it dear, having faithfulness

Featured Faith

Don't bark against the harmful
Not too loud
Symphony with love and joy
Kindness
Planted flowers
Through compassion

We've walked the path
It hurt like hell
Waking up in the morning feeling sluggish
Hung and on over
Clouded judgment, inhibited
Hiding in closets
When all we were seeking was true belonging

How you feel is no mystery
If you are consuming to fit in
So come away from it
Give yourself time
Pretty soon,
when you lookup
You'll see yourself rising

Above all the madness
When they're trying to classify you with mental diagnosis
Because of all the noise surrounding you
Blasting away common sense
Where do the senses stem and extend from?
Operations of hurtful, blind, settings

Have you witnessed the fireflies
That beam and can be lured in with artificial light
When all they needed was to be free next to a bonfire

So make a smore
Share yourself
With friends and a charcuterie board
Here comes the end of the false war

Be with peace
Here is the offering
You are the light beaming

And they will look and feel confused,
"How can they know so much?"
But little do they know,
intuition is a valued treasure
Embedded from the heavens

Don't be upset, how we figured you out
Spend your time now, acting right

<u>Peak Jubilee</u>

Focus and bring collaboration
20% within the population
Grow
Give chances
Take their idea even if it's not what you wanted

The odds are in their favor
Indeed it is,
"Where is the proof?"
Well,
can't you see them still breathing?

You are not alone, you who feel down
Come here
Be uplifted
Loved
Beyond

Put in the time
Get creative
Express yourself
Even here in this silence
Depression mitigated

Give me your hurt,
to roam in peace,
having less fear

You are not alone
You have a gift within
Believe in the heart and soul
Trust here
Beating the odds forever more

Aim to build, nourishment
Not just for your own home but community

It's going to take all of us to put aside selfishness
And trust one another to feel transcendence

We gain a lot more than just our own fortune,
when we lead with love out in the open
Solving not dissolving
The riddle of existence, no longer falling

Come, live in heaven and integrity
Doing right by all your neighbors near

Return of the Titans

Keep your eyes high
Above the screaming of the hurt
Washing love all over it

And when it feels helpless
Here comes the soaring
Grace
Spirit
Lifting higher
Beyond the world
Easy mornings

So do different
Fill a cup with joy
Pour out the hate and judgments

Pour it out
Yuck
'Toxicity wont enter the blood'

Products or opinions
Hear this now,
in the heart space "there is only loving"
Prism shining
Enduring

Be

At times the tests aren't about the subjects taught in school
They may be emotional
A heat of argument, miscommunicated
So learn conflict resolution

Give soft eyes
Body posture that shifts
More than just the mood
Holding hands
Sharing respect

We're friends here
Be kind and gentle
Smile at their effort

They're passionate
Speaking
To feel validated
Even when they're uttering false narratives
Against their own selves
Not understanding life of true oneness

Shift, just listen intently
At times, they don't care for the given wisdom
They will only want to hear themselves speak out
Even mock you to your face, behind closed doors
Because of the programming

Do they not know how much they are leaking?
Through actions and behaviors
Micromessages

So nod and smile
Gentle, with grace
It is okay, forgiven

All will have to fight the wars, being childish
Until they realize the value of peacefulness
And those who came to them with warnings

Toll Taken

They laid their hands on you
I know
You were not meant to feel that hurt
Giving purple and pink imprints

Affecting in ways unseen
Took years to undo
Hurt manifestations
Making you wander,
in environments that were aiming to take you down under

Oh, I know hurt
Which you didn't deserve
Trust, to give it up when the time comes
Hurtful memories, replaying
That had kept surfacing

The time has come
The time is now

Give away those hurtful things
Release them
And feel different

Grow yourself and set them an example
Showing even in hard times,
we can aim to be gentle

Do not despair and feel loathing,
replaying false opinions
Leading to feel sickened,
within consciousness and the heart space
Feel now for yourself,
even this author has been through it
Leading out doing different

You'll need to be so brave
Here is the honest answer
Forgive, especially through the hurting
Making all the difference

Hold no resentment in your vibrancy
Refuel the cells, feel the sunshine rays

Go free now
Choose love
And pretty soon
You will feel, yourself growing,
more peaceful

<u>We can</u>

Love is a power
Covers you in times of a challenge

Don't doubt it

Not romantically
Higher above
Trust the walk
Trust the answer
Trust yourself even when it doesn't hum
Being the catalyst

When everyone conforms to willful blindness
But you choose to be more aware
Not over anyone
But the human condition,
for wisdom intuition

So see others near
Just as strong
Standing up for the truth and love out in the open

At times they'll need you
Fear is a coward
So take this strength
Pour it into your consciousness

A new way
A change from diluted perceptions
Changing behavior
Walking to the true treasure
Away from blind consciousnesses

Home
Felt
Harmony
Belonging

A heavenly kingdom

Focused Fortune

Today is already history
The present is seeded
So plant the day
Win the fortune

Give yourself homework
Even when you've graduated
Break topics down, learn all you can

Biology
Architecture
New homes
Ecosystems
Even developers
Building virtual infrastructure

Learn, and be the change
And forgive them, those who've sowed false narratives
Thinking they were on the right side, feeling just
Justifying to research
Covert operations
Even gossip

Value education it raises us up
Developing points of reference
Diverse operations
Empathy
In organizations

Be wise,
Who surrounds you?
Go within, feel what surfaces

Is it the truth, clear conscious
Or does it feel like intimidation stemming from coercion

You can have mortals all around giving advice,
"If you don't do it this way, this is the outcome"

Where is thy faithfulness, where is it?
How many will have to blossom and bloom,
for you to start believing

Giving the best a small seat,
calling them low hanging fruit
Look now here, who's harvesting who?
Fruits of spirit ringing true

Tongues be silenced
Thinking the same could not happen to their own kids

But this author bigger than armies combined,
pushed through all the hate to help and love thy neighbors
So hear, "who is really more graceful?"

A new time and era begun
This land is home of the brave and courageous
Here she is winning
Blooming
Beyond all who doubted,
false belief and narratives in consciousness

Thinking opinions were required for validation
The most high has seen and spoke to her
Mortal opinion mean so little,
when you've got faith from the heavens

If you even think about saying an unkind word to her,
or anyone else
Know, tongues will be silenced

She sat there while they probed
Poking at her, trying to derive reactions
Little do they know the strengths it takes
To look past their small and selfish ways,
that send out hate

Resonant Aura

*Not talking about the problems but resolving them
Spending more time being the solution*

*Every book has an author
But who's message is coming from the highest?*

*Learn due diligence
Check-in
Who assumes the worst?
Is it this or learned mistruths?*

*Learn the outlook
What's the view?
Propagated misunderstanding
But this new symphony,
bringing peacefulness*

Giving context
Beyond the assumptions
When all the cues are present
People quitting and things surfacing
Senate hearings

Often times,
people can get caught up in the cycle of production
Even when they know what they're making isn't helping

So try your best to understand intention
And grow
Be brave not to be a criminal
Admitting the truth

Oh, who's driving initiatives?

Festivals full of plastered ideologies
Making others worship false gods and prophets

Walk in it and see for yourself
They'll even track your IP
Sending scams and fears

Is it excitement or entrapment
Justice, what's the truthful answer?
Thinking the heavens can't see through
And cancel with a storm or two

So trust, we're reeling out thousands
And they will be so upset
They couldn't squander life

Now brimming this truth
For those who climbed out to be whistle-blowers

Oh they'll try to stall
But the lord knows,
it was only allowed, to bring about the truth

*This whole time, they thought they had you fooled
But little do they know
Who's replacing who*

*They saw what was enabled and stayed silent
But heed and hear these angels who came across the oceans*

*Learning the lifestyle
Gauging what spirits here in the Americas are subjected to
Surely it is not the truth*

<u>Shimmer Glimmer</u>

Why do you feel agitated?
Take inventory of the consumption
Differentiate

Identify inputs
Elements
From gratification to acetaldehydes
Shortest path

Even when our souls feel the connection
Not building barriers or walls
But tearing down the falsehoods
Reminding of truth
Within the heart
Spirit of design
Away from false perceptions

Egoship
Who's on the titanic?
Without a sound deduction

This won't lie to you
No faults
Know you've got the opportunity here
To choose love

Grow seeing inner essence
Choosing different
Be welcomed to heaven
Into responsibility

This book is straightforward, required to be
At times,
being straightforward is what's healthy

If they ever try to take another life
It's going to be a dark day in hell

So hear this loud and clear
Steer away from the souls of spirit
Those who choose love with integrity
Even those who have done mistakes
The truth is seen
And if you keep probing, here will come a reckoning

This is your warning

Joint Practice

Won't give up on you
Won't,
at least not this author

But there is an army of us out here,
even in the unseen

With all the mistakes and wrong-doings
Giving second chances
Forgiving

Won't give up on you
Even when the whole world walks out
Believe it
You will make it
Flourish

Out of hurt into newness
Letting go of offensive behavior

Keep at it, be brave
Day in and day out
They can't count you out
Cheering for you

Reassurance
The power of the one
One more day
Climbing higher

It could be in school doing homework
Or getting clean from toxicity
Learning a skill
At times, it's hard to see longevity

But give yourself time and adapt
Grit Gears
Perseverance

Be aware of the inner narrative or dialogue
Sync without sinking
Focus on gratefulness

Exceptional Fortress

You can give up on 1 thing
When the times comes
You've got to let go

The one thing that is holding you down
That surfaces time and time again
Making you feel inhibited,
from moving forward

Give it up
Give it
Away into the open

Why let it hold you down?
How many more years will it take away from you?
Cycling

All is required is a seed of faith
To know,
when you let go, the universe will catch you

Durable Closure

You deserve different
Betterment

Oh look, on ahead
What do you see?

Look again
Look up
New vision, truth perspective

Oh look
Do you see yourself?
Above the mass of destruction

Look beneath under your feet
All those hurtful things
Dissolving

You can
You can
You can
Be one of the lucky ones

Choosing faith over fear
Persevering
Even when all they do,
is in agreement reaffirming, falsehoods

Lord knows, what changes the tides
Makes all the difference, being different
Standing out

And giving, a helping hand
Not sending,
guilt or fear into the consciousness of the beloveds here

High Caliber

Have heart
Have courage
Have faith
As adversity passes

On and through
Walk
Each scene
Feeling wholesome

Instantaneous
Sponge the value of truth
Get going
Don't live in the suffering

Study it
Never ruminate
Why did it happen?
What was required?
Here is a clue
Virtues
Values
Sponge the water

Oh it's that easy
Those hard experiences
Be made soft
Bringing healing to the infrastructure

A reflection of habits
What's practiced in the private

It's not reflective of the soul
Only learned from established environments
Prompted
That were allowed
Even when ethics was passed down

So take this antidote
Clarity
Wisdom truth
Don't let the hurt experienced by others, keep you

Free yourself
Unshackle
Those habits trying to keep you down under
From those who could not see in kindness,
only deep pockets

__Hard Love__

That's it
Uncover

Hear

A healed heart
Will always look out for the best interest of another

Even when they separated us
And gave little to us
Through populated feeds,
making you rationalize different

But this will, will lead out
Not bleeding out
Through the uncharted and unknown
Away from the darkness
Leaving a light on

Love
Endurance
Steadfast
Grit Gears
Secret Sauce
"No fear"
Persevering

Be love, beloved
Through love, anything is possible

Platonic Solid

Do you hear the spirit
Lifting us
Drumming beats, onward

Cheering on, getting over hurdles
Choosing love over the hurting

Choose your battles
Be wise
The war we're fighting
Is not seen
In consumption, think backwards

Addiction or cancer
What are we battling?

Is it convenience or a good time
Energy in production,
reinforcing hospital creations

A harmful mood
Or emotions
Enticing, to seek comfort through the senses

Rise friend, see it
This is helping away from dead endings

You are so important and loved
Trust we're about to shift real fast

And bring about awareness
And all those who doubted will soon see

Trust, it will be done
Rule the day
Emperor
Live in peaceful offerings
Away from the partying
While we build healthy and safe belonging

Mysterious Enigma

There are hidden things
Beyond the public sphere
Even in the technological
Tugging at your nerves
Suggestions

But replicate this
Awareness
Even with all that's available
Take your access and power back

'No thanks'
Choosing different
Living out your truth
No gossip

Speak kindness and give a helping hand
When division is propagated
Do the alternate

If enticed by fear, practice faith
If hate is uttered, be silent
Feel the magnitude of choosing different

Change the tides
If the storms find you
-Smile-
You are making the true fortune

And soon, they'll think you're an alien
Why don't they comply or conform
Fall in line to do more harm

Better believe we're more than eyes can perceive

The most high sees
Few are chosen
To bring forth authentic healing

This author had felt the whirlwind of it
Hurricane and storms
But even through the terrain
Steady pace given, to help and give encouragement

So don't doubt the effort
See this giving truth and wellness
You've got great powers from spirit
Capital gains is not truth foundation

Ask for guidance from consciousness, before you deduce
And pretty soon you'll be walking the golden path too

Seventy Seven

This author came distances
And with exposure made mistakes
She felt so sad for it all
And spirit came through lifting her higher
Showcasing dreams
'It's not your fault'

So be aware and cautious
Things are not what they seem
Get yourself near the tree

Don't feel ashamed or try to wear a mask
Be brave to be authentic
Energy higher than ever calculated
Calibrated
Getting into the sweet pocket

Being accountable and responsible
Living in integrity isn't hard
What will hurt is going against
Recycling harm

It's okay
'Yikes, I fell again'
That's okay
We'll get back up
Dust ourselves off
Begin again

Trust it
Choose integrity
Even if the misinformation made you choose the wrong options

Time is on your side
Indeed is
It is given from the heavens
Feel nourished

As you develop
Learn ethics
Some topics wont be so obvious
When everyone is worried about taxes

Do your counts and be cool
Smile
Here
High five, sixth sense

Hmm...

Just because you're exposed to it
Doesn't mean it's credible

Observe intently
How will spirit guide?
Will it have you following disrespect?

Each person is living it out
Either what to do or refrain from
So be mindful
Take time to process
Being of good moral character

What is in your exposure?
Even videos can be orchestrated
Neural networks
Deployed
Designs with false headlines
Click bait
Just to entice temperaments

Be slow not to hast into reactions
Ask questions and get curious

Better yet, learn the internet
SEO, research gate
What's each article referencing?

Why need spies
When it can be automated and collected

Social media
Who is populating narratives?

Projecting what they do
To later be suggested to
Algorithms of a function or ethics
To give, proper guidance

How is technology serving the most high?
Is it the users fault or an enticement?
Reinforcement

Where is the sanctions?

Prudent Truce

Peace won't sell
Because it fulfills the soul
The modesty that isn't after selfishness
Better believe we have arrived to our heaveness

Those who will change the tides
Oh sea and harbors
In the infrastructure

They see us coming
So smile if you've bought this
Smile friend, see where she is now
No accident, a new era begun

You and your children will be looked after
We will not quit
Love and hope
Seeing others worthy
Their children playing safely

Whether they're 7 or 25
We're building away from a false belonging

Oh trust we're out to build different
And pretty soon you will notice
Nature, this nation
Blooming
Within its heart and soul out in the open, blessings

Eternal everlasting

Good Gracious

Even with a projected picture of being financially limited
Mortals who say,
"It's not possible, you're going to be homeless"
"You're out of your mind,
if you ever thought you can make a worldwide difference"
"We doubt love can change anything"

This love prevails
Love, will speak louder than any words

Love, will heal every nation

This will, of love, will never give up on those worthy
Even throughout centuries

In the physical or spirit
It's true
Intuitive
Making it flourish

Giving hope
Even when they dose you with fear and false beliefs
Know, you are not alone in this sphere

We don't care what the statistics say
All you who doubt will soon see

What touches the heart, touches all of us
And you too will become more spiritual

Believing we can
Get through
On together
Friend to friend
Heartfelt rhythm
Through each page written

Forgiving, in tough times
Being kind, taking inspired action

Stellation Constellation

Won't give up on you
Impossible
Even with all that's going on

Won't give up
Even if the world walks out
Believing and trusting within the heart

Choosing life
Climbing up above
Rising
Higher standards

Setting up others for success
Higher order
Conduct of respect,
"No, won't let toxins enter bloodstreams"

Don't throw in the towel
Not in the soul or spirit
It makes all the difference

Positive attitude
Beyond the passive altitude
Keep at it
Day in and day out
One assignment after another

Showing up for humanity, a source family
One skill after the next
Seeing through the continents becoming legendary

The more you learn
The more you'll see
Transform
Mental models
Growing empathy
Lifting the beloveds here

Scaling more than just software
Authentic clean consciousness

Quantum Entanglement

This they can't replicate
Lived truths
Speaking
Through spirit within

Speaking up, rising
Giving a helping hand to those still falling
Waiting for their wings to break open

They're not allowed to replicate what's from the soul
Better believe we're scaling different

A wise alternative
Beyond the division or the fears
Flooding in feeds

New wirement
Here it is

Sown
Faithfulness courage
Brimming change

A resilient attitude
Adopted
From the most high
Changing standards

We will do different within our generation
We won't continue to speak or amplify the drama
Reassuring, to grow in development

And pretty soon people will hear the call
Telling them to learn health and compassion
Like those who come before
Left sayings,
"Be the change you wish to see"
"Have faith, no fear"
"Peace grows here"

Purple Lavender

It's a beautiful day
Even if the sunshine is hidden
Behind the clouds or the rain

The nutrients and energy still beaming through
As this written
Not buried

Trust sweet
All this happening
Changing tides
Even through the storms
Angels looking out for you

Look
This bought bringing about
Health and love
New guidance form

Be aware of consumption, it's in the details
And then witness what has replicated

Pay attention, little ones
Pretty soon, you will be giants

Memory Recall

Your feet will take you many steps
So will your mind
Moving across the plane

Exercise
Focus
At times it can be exhausting

Capacity and threshold
Stretched
Even muscles rip, when strengthened
Trusting instincts

Stronger than the seems
Don't be your own worst enemy
Just because others have spoken,
"Something is wrong with them, can't put my finger on it"

So let them keep their hands and energy to themselves
As we uplift the true ones

*Be a cheerleader to yourself and others near
Climb the ladder
Away from hurtful behaviors*

*We need you here
Choose
Health and clean moderate eating*

*Cheering you on
Even from afar
Don't feel discouraged*

*Build up
Strong body
Strong mind
Soulful resilience
You are not alone
Here, becoming
A legend*

Forge Ahead

At times we can cause frowns
Just as we receive the stimulus
But utilize the power
In the pause

What is this done or spoken enticed from?
Be curious
Stay observant

At times even that which is entertaining can lure you in
Away from empathy
Regression til you can't see
Everyone moving so emotionally

Love could be so irrational
Beyond common sense
A times, it will be what will help us win the war
As this given

*Not romantically
But humanity*

*To see past destruction and pain
Covering with healing
Forgiving ancestors*

*So never doubt the love given
Reminding manners
Friend, neighbor
Don't be enticed to speak ill intentions*

*The young is watching you
And pretty soon,
they'll be speaking the same about you*

*So be wise
Take inventory
What is your free expression in utterance*

Peace or fear?

*We've been given so much
Gracious
Efforts of the collective
Everyone is trying their best
At times, truth of reality is relative*

Honorable Gene

The people around you may not always be honest
Lies require preservation
Stemming from fear not spirit
At times, just to fit in

Lies can fester
Like an infection
Secrecy
If we don't take accountability to choose honesty

Lies can erode the fabric of society
Just to consume and have deep pockets
Burying the surfaced experiences

So answer this high call
Living with integrity, being honest
Forgive yourself and others too
The high supports

Teach in ways
Be gentle with who might still operate
Self-preservation is a nervous habit
Rationalization can shift perspective
Justifying

We'll need all the kindness we can get
From within our vibrancy
So others may come to understand,
all is forgiven, if you choose to do different

Here and forever more
No need to fight
Soul connection
Will speak out in the open,

"All is forgiven"

Grit Gears

Be brave through the storms
At times you'll be alone
Know you are not lonesome
Made wholesome

Even the author
Had to sit and sleep in the cold while writing this
Expressing,
"So what, if I eat a can of soup or go days without eating food.
Victory tastes sweeter"

*Look now, how far she's made it
She had spoken out in the open,
"Won't give up on them. Even if they took my brother.
Here there are others, who still need heartfelt overcomings"*

Believe, you too can make a difference

*Even when you perceive having little
Find a way, lead with love in the open*

*See in a day or two
Do the work, so it helps grow
True fortune
In hearts and temples*

*All false narratives will come to naught
Convince yourself doing the right thing will set new sails*

*Look up and look within
How the best of all that's ever been done
Sings
Not sting*

Truth of harmony shared
Reminding to not feel puzzled today

Have heart
Have courage
Have faith
Over fear
Becoming fear-less

Have hope
Take it
It is freely given

You are full of life and reassurance
Oceans and the rivers
Currents beyond the electric
Sacred

Transcendent Affections

*You are in the light
At times the mind can keep you feeling the dark
The thoughts held and occupied the mind
They're not true or kind*

*Evict them
Say goodbye
Send them a thank you card
For having taught you
What not to do*

*You've got to care
You've got a soul within
Think of the little child beside you
How special are their little feet?
That keep going the distance
You are like them, no different*

You've got special gifts
Don't let what happened or is happening make you doubt
Yourself or others
Lift higher
Not physically but within,
spirit connection
Always wins

Get up off that ground
Get out of that cage
Break that barrier today

Let the spirit unleash
All the potential
Kinetic
-Deep breathing-

This is written to encourage you
Do different with good
Try your best not to fight those who hurt
Give love

It will help create their point of reference,
to doing different

*Remind them what is from true source
At times, it'll mean walking away
Strive so they can learn,
not against them, but to inspire*

*You've got lots to build
And reassurance to give*

*Those little ones or the vulnerable
Needing you in ways unseen*

*Needing a helping hand
So feel this, here, reaching*

Faithful Endurance

When life gives you curve-balls
Or lemons
Get ready
Make something of it

A celebration
Sweet lemonade
Striking out
Home run
Here to our kingdom

Trust yourself
The guidance within
There are hidden things behind the scenes
Speak kindly and be poised

Better yet, silent
Babyling will lead to suffering

Observe
Look at them
Move
Pay attention

Sponsorship
What's the lesson
Figure it out

So you may do the opposite
The unexpected
Sow love and kindness
Teaching them an example

Sown resonance
For the ones here
The ones making peace in this sphere

Bout' Time

Fear can be scary
May cloud opinions
Fear can get you in a rut
Sometimes hiding from past mistakes

Fear can be scary
It can grip you
Just to agree with those beside you

Fear can be scary
Sending heat
Making one feel frantic

Fear can be scary
Directed to make one impulsive
Diluting perception
Buying

Fear can be scary
Making one lash out
Speaking ill of the ones they love
False perceptions

Fear can be scary
It can paralyze
But pretty soon
Trust
Love will undo the harm

Whispering,
"Fear is a liar, it won't take us,
we're full of heart and faithfulness"

Here we come
Glowing
See us winning
Away past harmful opinions

You've got to give it up, for the way it works
A divine hand, in it all

<u>Synonym Characteristics</u>

This heart fails you not
We love you beyond the words or fiscal status
Even when materialistically down under

Fear not
Love will sweep in
Bringing you up
On your feet
Even if you weren't raise well

Fear not
Dear friend
Here we come
Not one, but throughout centuries favoring you

Don't waste time in rumination
Dinking of someone else's poison

What has the imagination done to little kids?
Make them hide beneath their beds

So crush that fear
-wahm-
Won't feel ashamed
Will no longer be misguided

*This is true,
loved unconditionally*

*Don't feel down or frown
Be brave
Be courageous
Take this strength
Plant it in your mind and consciousness*

*Even if you have to act it out
Superhero pose
While you undo those doubts
A clearing
Cleaning
Within the mind
Making a new garden*

*Have no fear
Live with integrity
You will soon see
Authentic flavors, may give tougher skin
Getting rid of the blemishes*

Drum Roll

When you feel diluted
Full of emotions
Perhaps drinking of mischief
Away into the night
Away from benevolence
Cycling with reinforcement to false belongings
Sending you out into wilderness
Notice the natureness
How many storms were there?
How well did you sleep the night before?
Every time you tried to attend a space,
stemming from harmful productions

Break the cycle
Chain-breaker
Spend time being responsible
Seeing the patterns
No matter the probes
Aimed to make you take off your spiritual robe

You've got a force field
And angels, as this
Seeing up above the chaotic

Protecting in ways unseen
Trust who you are walking with, she is your beloved

Has the sun not been designed?
Even the earth
Fire can't put out the water
Better know your making
Seventh heaven sown
Early on

So be upright
Peacefulness will require strength
Earning a place amongst the people

It isn't only about manifestations,
of what you can have,
Earn by looking out for brothers and sisters

Don't let the marketing or wars
That are physically seen or hidden
Entice you to revolt
Do with love and peacefulness

Mindful and strategic
Speaking truth
In ways that change hardened hearts and opinions

<u>Focal Point</u>

You don't need to win a false war
Grow intellectual and wise

Every time you win, a new learning
Is the mystery that makes humanity flourishes

Ask yourself,
"How can this help? Me or the one beside me?"
Being honest

Unleash the creative genius
No faults

Aim to hear the symphony and see the orchestration

Sophia

What's brewing?
Is it something reassuring?
That fulfills

What can we do?
Rise higher or get even?

Sit outside and lookup
High above
Beyond the horizons

Each person on the other side deserves quality
In health and spirit dear

Perception can make you doubt who's next to you
But this series of love will undo raveling and fulfill you

Truth
True love shared
All it takes is for you to remain open to hear the message

Be wise, not naive
Be open to do kind deeds

In shelters of safe haven
Within the heart
Connected to our friends in neighborhoods

It doesn't matter how many times we will face it
Love is the answer

So forgive them those who fall
In misperceptions and illusions
Showcased
Projected from consumption

Spirit connects
Sending love out in the open
To you and another
Lifting higher
Forgive a father
A mother too is special
Clothed and vulnerable from what she had to face

So grow wise
Be strong
Protecting humanity
Will serve life
Beyond the times
Even if it's hard to get along

Strawberry Lemonade

They can try to squeeze you,
or have you against the wall
Just to see how you will react,
when you have nothing

So hear
-smiling-
"You won't find the true ones hating"

Even when they're probed with tragedy and deceptions
Only growing wise with insights
Sending love out in the open

You'll see through us
Leading the way
Better believe
Those who hate
Are the ones beneath

Fear not, we are on the same side
Full of light
Better get on the side of the most high

Be still, friend
And hear this roar

Those who try to corner the vulnerable
Will soon have to answer

The ones in heaven are beating the drums
Pretty soon you will feel

Morality
We will not be made demoralized
To hate the one beside us

So if you're propagating the lies
Know
Your time is coming
A reckoning

So steer away
You've got time
This is your opportunity

Be forgiven,
if you answer with love to this warning

Erg Origins

The person across from you may be down
Clouded from within
Keep your feet to yourself
Don't kick a person whos fallen

Their inner experience is sensitive
Feeling distressed
So extend a helping hand
Lift them up

You've got great power
Encouragement
Each time you look out for your fellow
Is an extra credit

Not financially
Or in the classrooms of school
But in spirit heaven,
aiming to live out the good

How educated are you?
In the ego or the heart
Feel the power of love
Lifting one another out of burials

Dear friend we're giving you our hand
Grip, here
Away we'll pull you out

Look even in perception
It will change trajectory
Making moves in kindness is the mystery

Step up
Step on this
Above hate into loving

Smile you are not alone
It's hard to be forgiving,
because resentment is a tasty poison

It's not worth it
Let it go
Grow
To glow
Making a difference better than before

Don't doubt how this love will elevate
Success leaves a trail

Value set
Rising
Faithful not prideful

Chosen Determinism

They will come out of nowhere
Those who tell you to fear
Sinking ideologies
Telling you,
'Hate the one beside you,
and the government that protected you'

Be aware, of the mind
How it shifts assuming the worst
Sit in wisdom today

Witness

Distinguish opinions
Humility
Who's humble?
To know he's not better than another?

*Remember the coded spirit genetics
You really think they're not born worthy?*

*Look again, where are they now
Those of you who said they couldn't become anything*

*The justification in hate will never win
Sit back
And watch
Even when you try to collect information and data
Trying to piece the puzzle,
when you haven't even looked within you*

*It's okay, keep consuming this
And see for yourself*

*How a shift in perspective, will lead to have more love
Evolve
Not in consumption "More for me"
But what you will come to see
Is the true treasure shared
Stems of the heart and soul
Filling up, better fuel, hope sprinkled*

*Bread and oil
Fueled heart, loving endurance
Making a worldwide difference*

Tranquility

Smile so gentle
Shifting energy
From ego

Nourish
Don't fear
Even if your feet tremble

Stand tall
Be still
Through the lens
Compassion

Luxury
Not the one selling insecurity

A truthful gem
No longer hidden

Share, so it makes it clear to see
You are more than consumption of fear

Even when everyone pointed at behavior,
"Look at them, they're a lost soul"
Even then, not trusting the training
Soulful overcomings

So bet on the spirit of others
Even when it is not evident

Courage
Honor
Duty
Commitment
Integrity
Service

Don't you realize?
You won't scare them
Just building their confidence

It's not so easy identifying
Motives, values, beliefs, or intentions

The people love
Indeed they do
When the right actions are done by ALL of them

You will see a change
Think long term, foresight
How is technology propagating criminals?

Even when they rationalize their hurtful behaviors,
in duress
High standards
Hard to establish

Who here started with proper guidance
Moving between homes
Barely getting healthy habits down
That keep a shiny smile

So forgive and be gentle
Even those who you've seen repeatedly
If it wasn't for basic camp,
some could have faced their path

So this is requiring empathy
Or a scholarship

Help give free education without loopholes
Limiting excuses

Spring Sane

The complexities are that
Complex
But trust those who see and witness
Reinforcing positive habits
Identifying elements

Nature and nurture
Away from dichotomies
Because they tell you it can only be this or that
V.S.

What is the picture?

Someone always against another
Where is our heaven?

Interconnected
Spirit
Truthful
Sweetness

The little ones striving
The ones that trusted the education
Believing they can be themselves

To later be lured, towards harmful productions
"peace, love, unity, respect"
In masses, pride festivals
Blaming it on Adam and Eve

False ideologies, conducted out in the open
Introducing them to light-working and magic

Tapestries of false gods
Reinforcing irresponsible belief systems

Stones and spells
Thinking the heavens not see
The toxicity

This here, is about to dissolve
The dark and harm from ever again coming about
To the children of heaven in the open

Where is the life of truth vitality?
Where is it?
Are they who lead blind and still asleep?

So let this be your warning

If you don't change,
the ones who made it out are healed
Pretty soon you will see who's replacing who

Don't squandered the sacred opportunity
To do right by all,
not only yourselves of what you deem is sweet

Look now, they're moving on in
And they will bring a different refreshing prism

Joy Triumph

Challenges, yeah so what
Look inside our heart
True strength
From up above

You won't even feel it anymore
That which is aimed to misguide you
You will see right through them too

Look at these wings
Angels being born
Armor of love proven
No longer misunderstood or mistaken

When we're walking with the unseen
Bringing faithfulness here

You who read this, you are not alone
Don't let a few poems written, for those who need to heed,
make you think we're talking about you

We're giving them warnings
So use the this time to make changes

Don't be frightened or scared
We're holding the force

Do what you can
Help yourself up
Even those beside you
Develop good character

Lookout for your well-being
Whether your 8 or in high school
Walking into nursing homes

Don't feel alone
Trust we're building
Bringing true love
Family
Sacred foundations

Don't doubt our connection
Love prevails

Feel reassured and hopeful

Be calm
Trust
These written words helping from up above

<u>Mighty Will</u>

The author was self-centered,
because of what was presented
But spirit lifted
After the age of maturity,
35, leadership

So be patient with the young
They're growing into becoming
It takes time
Even with all the screen wirements

The best you can do
Is give plenty within their tools
Empathy and compassion
A conditioning
A way to see, modesty

Second sight
So they don't inject or feel peer pressured
To fit in, when they are born worthy

Even with all the marketing showcasing,
skewed projected modeling

Brotherhood

*The audacity
Of what's spoken here*

*Do not be taken back
Be propelled to do different*

*With love and kindness
Looking out for your fellows*

*Talking with respect
Better yet, don't target*

*It's so easy to feel prideful,
to get more in your pockets
Thinking what you do is truth norm
When all was needed was to set high standards*

*How special is this?
Summing it up
The author having nothing to gain
Putting your children's feelings first,
leading with love*

*Trying to protect you and your family
When all they tried to do is misguide hers over money*

Even when hurt was given
Even belittlement and mockery
Sending hateful energy without a sound deduction

So humble
And brave
She was still aiming to protect you within her heart space

Looking out for your best interest
Not of deep pockets, spending her last dollar

But even thee had expressed
Don't aim to seek treasures in the world but up in heaven

Do you see what is being manifested?

Truth of soulful connection
So you may enter the kingdom come
And be able to operate in heaven function

Lucky We

Your shoe size grows
So does your spine with nerves

Oh the nerve
Aligned posture
Character built
Won't sit on the sidelines

Speaking kindly
Integrity

Writing with ink, even with tattoos
Coming from spirit
Connection

Rationality can make you do wild things
When you are cornered or have little
Don't fall for it
Even if your credit score falls with it

Do with integrity
Win the war
Raise yourself
In frequency to love

You won't ever need to utter any words
The energy will be felt as soon as you walk in

A warm heart, so true
Growing to cover those hurt, innocent, and vulnerable

It's going to piss of the hate
But put a smile on your face
It's good to have friction
Giving fuel to elevate nations

It's okay, give grace

And pretty soon other will feel the change
Mirror neurons
Magnetic
Force-field
Into the wholeness

Yee Wee Knee

See how difference of an opinion,
can lead to goodness

That which doesn't hold anything against you,
or over your head
Allows you to speak truth and be made righteous by choosing
different

Notice the opinions coming from the mind
Or the heart
Either beaming from spirit or absorbed from earthlings

The audacity
Yes
Here it is, again
"My friends are not for sale"
This is victorious

And pretty soon
A ticket given

Not for the sake of products or service
But humanity into the sacredness

Lifting life
Held higher
Given a fair chance
To bloom in understanding

What have we designed?
We better remain humble
Or feel the bubble

Tokens of products or service
Need to be scoped for health and wellness

Celebrations
Leading life
Higher consciousness than before

River Pebbles

Listen to this
Loving heart
You are capable
Persevere

Don't give up, even if it feels like the end
Push get past it
Exercise
Condition the mind

Glass ceiling
Shattered
Breaking barriers
The imaginary impossibilities
And the odds
Misperceptions,
of those who thought it couldn't be possible

Have heart
You've got an infinite well

Dear friend
Take courage
Climb out of the darkness

It's possible

Carried Field

The violence is felt
Don't let the truth of senses
Be misperceived
When you're hungover laying in bed for days

Rejuvenate, consume different
Feeling confident

How are you fueling?
What do you pour inside of your spirit?
Even they who come around you with peer pressure

Build yourself authentic,
"No, thanks"
Won't subscribe to the poisoned ways

It's okay not to fit in
You're meant to stand out
So you can help others rise

Lead the uncharted path
Leave a trail
So others find the gold and silver
Beyond the crypto or the dollar
Pyramid schemes
Not sharing meals

Keen Force

You can make anything rhyme
Use the focused lens
Given to you from the beginning

You can put others down
Or let hearts grow wide
Pushing past vengeful ways, that send out hate
Or doing different to ensure,
other hearts are not broken

Smile, this is helping
Bringing evolution
Progress
To assume kinder

Away from hurtful happenings
As the heavenly is properly investigating

And all the ones that were persecuted,
be vindicated

And others realize,
who really was the hidden treasurer

Νίκη

Hurray,
for the days
Each woke up
Deciding, "This fight ain't over"
Winning the battle

The one's still in it
Feeling it
The inspiration
Beyond imagination

The one's pouring out
Love
Instead of prideful arrogance

The one's who came up
Even having little
When they had family, having fortunes

Reminding, there's more to the truth
Don't haste or fall into hasty judgments
Even when they tell you to turn your back,
on those who helped you

How is memory formed?
What's the recall?
Is it facts or emotions

What are we going to do now?
What? Tell me... Where is thy faithfulness?

Are we going to let go of all the harmful conditioning's?
Remembering spirit essence
Not false impressions

Even with all that's been passed down before,
speaking over material objects, that can lure the vulnerable

Will we value money and attention above connection?
Or may we have humility to no longer be pointing the finger?

Will we get greedy to put toxicity on the shelf or in feeds?
Or decide the return on investment is not worth it?

Will we slide into hasting, misjudgments, classifying, clusters?
Or will we offer grace, reminding others
"You are okay, here's a new opportunity"

Will we belittle with rolling eyes, speaking unkind?
Or will we rise being wise, shaking hands?

What will we do? Who here has power?
To change from within, bringing a new foundation

Beyond the horizons

"Never ascribe to malice,
that which is adequately explained by incompetence"
- Hanlon's Razor

Book soundtrack: **Guardian - Philipp Beesen**

About the Author

Farah has continued her legacy writing series 'To you From you' by sharing the fourth installment, 'Grit Gears'. This book was written Spring of 2024, during a challenged inflated economy. She aimed to publish 'Grit Gears' to inspire others to choose love and peace regardless of the storms of adversity and present circumstances, with media showcasing fears and wars.

As she blooms again, Farah shows the readers the power and possibilities of choosing to plant seeded goodness with kind intentions in the lives of those around her, leading with love. This bloom is aimed to bring mindful awareness, encouragement, and upliftment. We hope you enjoyed this series, be encouraged to share the publications with anyone who may need it.

About the Publisher

Rwh Publishing LLC was established in 2023 to publish creative content by artists that aim to uplift humanity and change lives for the better.

If you resonate with this message, please help share this with those who need it.

A portion of the proceeds from this book will be utilized to develop an infrastructure that aids individuals to feel grounded and centered, contributing to mind, body, and soul alignment along with strengthened character development.

Thank you for your support!

www.ingramcontent.com/pod-product-compliance
Lightning Source LLC
Chambersburg PA
CBHW020333010526
44119CB00002B/53